Contents

Some words are shown in bold, **like this**.
You can find out what they mean by
looking in the glossary.

Dazzling diamonds

▲ This diamond weighs more than 15 grams (half an ounce). It was cut from the Lesotho Promise, the largest diamond found so far this century.

They sparkle and shine. They give off colourful flashes of light. They are harder than any other substance on Earth.

Diamonds are some of the most sought-after objects in the world. They are also some of the most expensive. Diamonds are valuable in part because they are **scarce** (rare).

You probably know what a diamond looks like. But there are many things you may not know about diamonds. How did they form? Where are they found? How can you tell how much a diamond is worth? And why is a diamond linked with love? Read on to learn the amazing story of diamonds.

Stop, thieves!

Diamonds are worth a lot, so it is no wonder people try to steal them. One of the biggest attempts to steal diamonds took place a few years ago. In November 2000 a group of robbers came up with a plot. They planned to steal 12 diamonds from the Millennium Dome in London. The diamonds were worth £334 million. One of the diamonds was called the Millennium Star.

The thieves planned to crash into the Dome on a bulldozer and then grab the diamonds. It would have been the biggest jewellery theft ever. But police learned of the plan early. When the thieves broke in, the police were waiting for them. The big jewellery theft was prevented!

▼ Camera footage shows a man breaking the case that held the Millennium Diamonds. Four men were given long prison sentences for trying to steal them.

Where diamonds come from

▲ This is pure carbon in the form of graphite.

Most diamonds formed two to three billion years ago. They formed deep inside Earth's **mantle**. The mantle is the middle part of Earth that lies between 35 and 2,900 kilometres (22 to 1,800 miles) below the surface. Pressures are very high in the mantle. Temperatures are high, too – about 4,000°C (7,232°F).

How diamonds formed

The process of diamonds forming began with a tiny grain of pure **carbon**. Carbon is one of the most common substances on Earth. All living things are partly made of carbon.

The heat and pressure in the mantle fused (joined) layers of carbon onto the carbon grain. This created a very tightly linked, or bonded, substance. The tight bonds make diamonds very strong and very hard.

Rising to the surface

Diamonds made it to the surface with help from volcanoes. When ancient volcanoes erupted, they spewed hot, melted rock from deep inside Earth. This melted rock is called **magma**. Sometimes the magma carried diamonds.

When the volcanoes died, the magma hardened. This left behind a carrot-shaped pipe of cooled magma in the ground. Some of these pipes contain bluish-grey rock called **kimberlite**. Wherever people find kimberlite, there is a good chance of finding diamonds.

Diamonds and . . . pencils?

What do diamonds and pencils have in common? Both contain pure carbon. The dark, flaky substance in a pencil that leaves a mark is called graphite. Graphite is another form of pure carbon. But it is much softer than diamond. The carbon in graphite is not bonded together as tightly as it is in diamonds.

▼ Diamonds formed much deeper within Earth than the Grand Canyon in the United States or even the deepest mine. They came to the surface when volcanoes erupted.

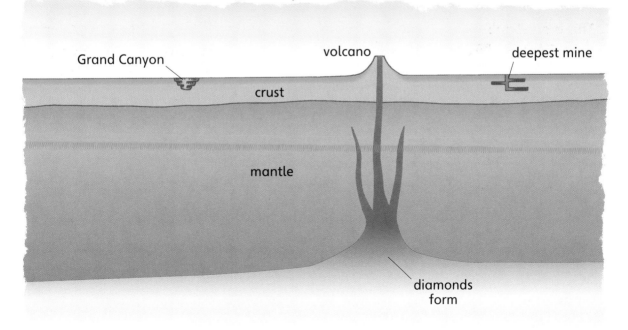

Grand Canyon

volcano

deepest mine

crust

mantle

diamonds form

Where diamonds are found

Most diamonds are found in kimberlite pipes. People get the diamonds out of the pipes through **mining** (digging in a pit or tunnel). The largest diamond **deposits** (natural build-ups) are in the countries of South Africa, Australia, Botswana, Russia, and the Democratic Republic of the Congo. Diamonds can be found in about 25 countries.

Sometimes diamonds make their way into rivers and streams. This happens through erosion. Erosion is when moving water, wind, or ice wears away rock or soil. The moving water leaves behind **alluvial** diamonds that are too heavy to be carried away. The word *alluvial* means "deposits made by flowing water".

▼ After a volcano dies, the magma that carries diamonds hardens into a kimberlite pipe that can be mined.

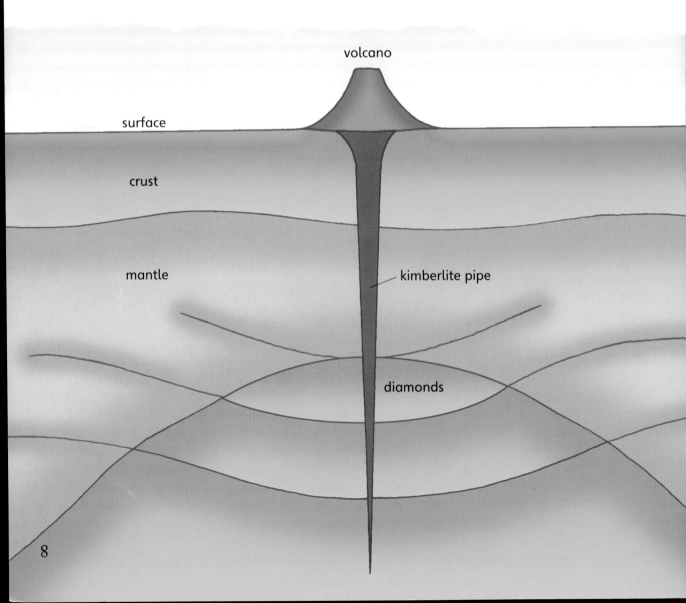

volcano

surface

crust

mantle

kimberlite pipe

diamonds

Rough, uncut diamonds look like rounded pieces of glass. Most are colourless. Some have a yellow tint to them. A few diamonds are red, pink, blue, green, or even black. High-quality coloured diamonds are worth a lot of money. These are called **fancy diamonds**.

▲ **This man is panning for diamonds in Kalimantan, Indonesia.**

Open pit mining

Mining of a kimberlite pipe begins with the creation of a large pit mine. (A mine is a pit or tunnel from which the diamonds are taken.) This is called open pit mining. Large shovels and lorries remove the rock material, one section at a time. Sometimes mine workers blast into the rock with explosives. Then they sort through the rock material, looking for diamonds. Diamond mining is tough, boring work. Even in the largest mines, people have to sort through about 250 tonnes (246 tons) of rock to find 0.2 of a gram (0.007 of an ounce) of diamonds of **gem quality**. It is like looking for a needle in a haystack!

From rings to drill bits

▲ A jeweller inspects the quality of a diamond.

Diamonds are prized gemstones. Gemstones (**gems**) are precious stones that can be cut and polished to a high shine. Gems are often used in jewellery.

Brilliance and fire

Diamonds sparkle and give off dazzling flashes of light. A diamond's sparkle is called **brilliance**.

The coloured light a diamond gives off is called **fire.** A diamond acts like a prism. A prism is a transparent (clear) object with three sides, which is used to bend light. Like a prism, a diamond breaks light up into a rainbow of colours.

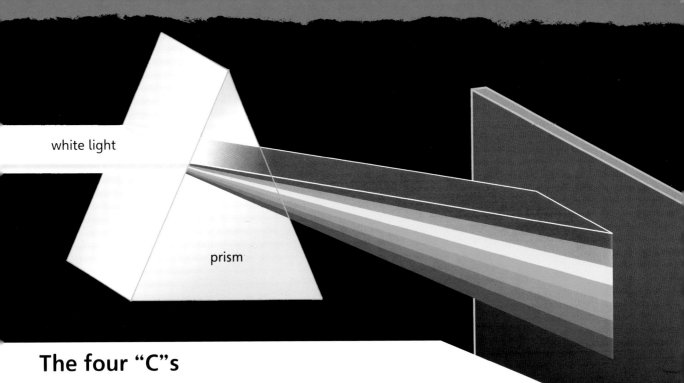

white light

prism

The four "C"s

Four things affect a diamond's worth. These are cut, colour, clarity, and **carat**.

Cut

A diamond can be cut in different shapes, but all shapes are made up of **facets**. A facet is a flat cut on a diamond's surface. Facets increase fire and brilliance by letting more light pass through. Diamonds may have about 50 to 200 or more facets.

Colour

Colourless diamonds are worth more than ones with some colour because colour decreases a diamond's fire. But high-quality, coloured **fancy diamonds** are worth more than colourless ones. They are especially **scarce**.

Clarity

Clarity is a measure of how clear a diamond is. Diamonds with higher clarity have fewer and smaller blemishes. A blemish is a mark. It can appear as a tiny crack or a cloudy area. Often you cannot see these blemishes with the naked eye. You need special equipment to see them.

Carat

A carat is a measure of a diamond's weight. One carat weighs 0.2 of a gram (0.007 of an ounce).

▲ A diamond acts like a prism that breaks white light into the colours of the rainbow.

▲ Diamonds like these are not good enough to be used in jewellery. They are used in cutting and grinding tools.

Diamonds in tools

Diamonds are not only used as jewellery. A diamond's hardness makes it very useful in tools. Only a diamond can cut another diamond.

Gem quality

Most diamonds found are not **gem quality**. This means their quality is too poor for jewellery. About 75 to 80 per cent of diamonds found are used in tools. Many of these diamonds are yellow, grey, or brown in colour.

Cutting tools

Because of their hardness, diamonds are used in many cutting tools. Drill bits are the long, thin cutting parts at the end of a drill. Drill bits with diamond dust are used to drill holes into very hard substances. Geologists (people who study rocks and earth) use steel bits with diamond tips to drill deep into the earth for rock samples. Some tools with diamond tips are used in making cars. Often grinding wheels are coated with diamond dust. Some diamonds are used to cut and shape other diamonds!

Harder than nails

Fingernails are no match for tough diamonds! Some nail files have a thin layer of diamond dust. These files stay sharp for a very long time.

FACT BOX

Diamonds at the dentist?
Have you ever been to the dentist to have a filling? If so, your teeth may have come in contact with diamonds. The drill bit on a dentist's drill is coated with diamond dust. Teeth are very hard, but diamond dust helps drill into them quickly – and, with luck, painlessly!

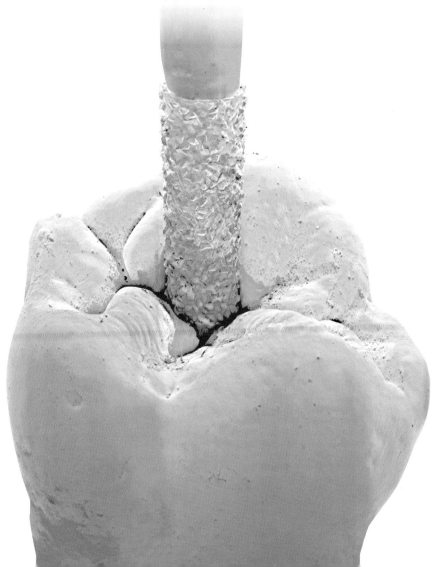

◀ This photo is magnified (enlarged) ten times. It shows a drill bit coated in diamond dust tunnelling into a tooth.

13

Diamonds in history

▲ An ancient Sanskrit text called the Garuda Purana includes advice about the form and value of diamonds. The Hindu god Vishnu gives this advice to Garuda, the bird that he rides.

For many years India was the only source of diamonds. Most of them were **alluvial** diamonds. Diamonds were first found in India in 400 BCE. We know this from written sources that mention clear, sparkly **gems**. The sources call the gems *vajra*. This is a Sanskrit word meaning "thunderbolt". Sanskrit was a language used in India at the time. Diamonds were probably described as thunderbolts because of the flashes of light they give off. The flash of light from a diamond looks like a flash of lightning.

400 BCE

India is the main world supplier of diamonds. This continues until 1700 CE.

1000 BCE   500 BCE   0

Diamonds in Europe

By the 1300s CE, Europeans were wearing diamonds in jewellery. These fine pieces of jewellery were mostly worn by **royalty** (kings, queens, and members of the royal court). But these diamonds were very small.

By the 1500s, royal jewellery began to feature large, sparkly diamonds. Jewellers had begun to put **facets** on diamonds. The facets made the sparkle and **fire** of the diamonds even more beautiful.

The king's gems

In the 1200s, King Louis IX (Louis the Ninth) of France passed a law. The law said that only the king could own or wear diamonds. This showed how rare and valuable diamonds were at the time. This paved the way for diamonds to be linked with wealth and royalty.

◀ This portrait of Queen Elizabeth I was painted in the late 1500s. The diamonds in her dress and crown were part of her display of wealth and power.

1200s CE	**1300s**	**1500s**
King Louis IX of France passes a law saying only the king can wear diamonds.	European royalty wear small diamonds in jewellery.	Royal jewellery begins to feature larger diamonds.

1200 CE   1300   1400   1500

Diamond discoveries

India was the main supplier of diamonds for hundreds of years. Then in 1725, major diamond **deposits** were found in the country of Brazil.

In the 1870s, people found large deposits of diamonds in South Africa. This led to a big increase in the supply of diamonds. For the first time ever, more than one million **carats** were **mined**.

Really that rare?

Are diamonds really as rare as most people think? That is very hard to tell. One very large company called De Beers owns much of the world's supply of diamonds. This allows the company to control how many diamonds are available. So, some diamonds are kept in large vaults, rather than in jewellers.

With fewer diamonds available to purchase, they seem rarer than they actually are. This makes them very precious – and very costly!

▶ Diamonds from this open-pit mine in South Africa were mined from 1870 to 2006.

1725

Major diamond deposits are found in Brazil.

1700

1800

Cecil Rhodes was an English businessman and politician whose activities in Africa made him very rich.

Cecil Rhodes

Cecil John Rhodes (1853–1902) was born in England. In 1870 he went to live with his brother in South Africa. Rhodes bought some land in an area known for diamonds. He soon became wealthy by operating diamond mines.

In 1889 he bought the Kimberley Mining Company. Rhodes called his mining company De Beers. At one time De Beers owned 90 per cent of the diamonds in the world. Today it still controls much of the world's diamonds.

Record cheque

Cecil Rhodes bought the Kimberley Mining Company for £4.5 million. At the time it was the largest cheque ever written.

1870
Cecil Rhodes goes to live with his brother in South Africa; he begins buying diamond mines.

1889
Rhodes buys the Kimberley Mining Company; he names the new company De Beers.

1900

Will you take this ring?

▶ It has now become a tradition for a man to give a woman a diamond ring when they get engaged.

In many countries today, diamonds are a symbol of love. A symbol is an object that stands for something else. But why are diamonds linked with love and marriage?

Rings for love

People have given rings as a sign of love for about 2,000 years. By the 4th century CE in Europe, it was common to exchange rings at a wedding. Many early wedding rings were plain gold bands.

The first diamond wedding ring was probably given by **Emperor** Maximilian I to his wife Mary, Duchess of Burgundy, in 1477. (An emperor is a ruler like a king.) Maximilian ruled the Holy Roman Empire, which at the time stretched from Italy into Germany and beyond.

A diamond is forever

Until the 20th century, only very wealthy people could afford to buy diamonds. In the late 1930s, diamond rings started to become more popular.

400

People in Europe begin to exchange plain wedding rings.

0   500   1000

A diamond company hired a New York City advertising firm to promote diamonds. The firm created advertisements about diamonds. The adverts ran in newspapers, in magazines, on television, and on the radio.

The campaign aimed to make more people buy diamond rings. It linked diamond rings to love and marriage. It showed young men buying their brides diamond **engagement** rings. (When people are engaged, they have agreed to get married.) The adverts sent the powerful message that "a diamond is forever". The adverts were a huge success. Diamond sales soared.

The following are the percentage of brides in recent years who have received a diamond ring	
Country	Percentage
United States	83%
Great Britain	75%
Japan	50%

How long is love?

a diamond is forever

◀ Romantic adverts like this one promoted the idea that diamonds are a symbol of love.

1477
Emperor Maximilian I gives a diamond wedding ring to wife Mary, Duchess of Burgundy.

1930s
Americans begin buying diamond engagement rings.

1500

2000

The trouble with diamonds

▲ Men sift for diamonds in a stream in Ivory Coast, Africa.

Many diamond **deposits** are in poor countries. In these places, finding a diamond can change a person's life.

Get rich quick?

Many people dream of getting rich by finding a diamond. So, they spend days or even years sifting through riverbed soil in search of **alluvial** diamonds. If they find one, they might get anywhere from £20 to a couple of thousand pounds for it.

This is a lot of money in a poor country. But it is nowhere near what the diamond is worth. A diamond that fetches £133 in South Africa might sell for about £26,000 in a wealthy country such as the United Kingdom. The people who cut and sell diamonds make far more money than the people who find or **mine** them.

Diamonds in films

Diamonds have a glamorous and exciting image. In a famous 1953 film, actress Marilyn Monroe sang "Diamonds Are a Girl's Best Friend". Later, Superman used his super strength to squeeze a lump of coal into a diamond on the big screen. Even today, film stars often show off glittering diamond jewellery in films and at awards ceremonies.

Worth less over time

Diamonds are different from most **gems** or precious metals. They do not go up in value. It is very hard to sell back a diamond to a jeweller. Those who do so often get far less than what they paid for it.

◀ The character played by Marilyn Monroe enjoys wearing diamonds in the film *Gentlemen Prefer Blondes*.

▲ Diamonds are found in the gravel of rivers in Africa. It may be illegal (against the law) to take diamonds like this.

Blood diamonds

Another problem with diamonds has to do with where they come from. Many Central and West African countries are unstable. The governments in power do not have control. In some cases, the governments are corrupt (dishonest).

In many of these countries, armed groups (groups with weapons) control the diamond mines. Working conditions in the mines can be awful. People may be forced to work long hours for little or no pay.

Sometimes children are forced to work in diamond mines. Often, in these places, money from the sale of diamonds goes to support violent groups. Diamonds from these sources are called **blood diamonds**.

Stopping the sale

Since the 1990s people have shown concern over blood diamonds. In 2002 the United States and other countries signed an agreement to end the sale of blood diamonds. It calls for certificates (papers) that ensure a rough diamond comes from a legal source.

However, the agreement has not solved all the problems. It is hard to tell where diamonds originally came from after they leave the country where they were found. In 2006 alone, about £15 million worth of blood diamonds from the Ivory Coast were sold through nearby countries. Violent, corrupt groups control parts of Ivory Coast where diamonds are found.

Stealing diamonds

Sometimes diamond mine workers try to steal a diamond they find. They may hide the diamond under their tongue or between their toes. If they are caught stealing, they may lose their job, get beaten, or worse.

▼ In some places, people with weapons are in charge of diamond mines.

23

Fake diamonds

▶ It is now possible to turn the ashes of dead people into diamonds for their loved ones to keep.

Because of the high cost of diamonds, people have searched long and hard for something to take their place. But few things have a diamond's sparkle or hardness.

A few substances in nature come close to diamonds. One is called cubic zirconia. It sparkles and throws off light the way diamonds do, but it is nowhere near as hard. A cubic zirconia **gem** costs much less than a diamond!

"Diamonds" from space

Another material similar to diamond is moissanite. In 1893 a French scientist called Henri Moissan was looking at some rock samples. The samples were from a **meteor**, a rock from space that landed on Earth. Moissan found a clear, sparkling, hard material in the rock samples. He thought it was a diamond.

Soon he realised he had a new material on his hands. Later the material was named moissanite, after Moissan. Today scientists have a way to create moissanite in the laboratory. Like diamonds, moissanite is used in both jewellery and tools.

More sparkle than a diamond?

A gem made of moissanite has more **fire** and **brilliance** than a diamond!

Human-made diamonds

Today it is possible to make diamonds. The US company General Electric first made **synthetic** (human-made) diamonds in 1955. They did it by using high temperatures and pressure on **carbon**. This is similar to what created real diamonds in Earth's **mantle** millions of years ago. Synthetic diamond material is mainly used in tools.

All that glitters

▲ The Imperial State Crown is part of the display of the Crown Jewels.

Diamonds still dazzle the eye and capture attention like no other **gem** on Earth. The Koh-i-Noor, Cullinan, Hope, Golden Jubilee, and Dresden Green diamonds are some of the largest and finest diamonds ever found.

Koh-i-Noor

This 106-**carat** diamond is now one of the British Crown Jewels. The Crown Jewels are worn by the king or queen during special events. The crowns, rings, and other pieces contain a total of 23,578 gems. The Imperial State Crown alone has 2,868 diamonds! Altogether the Crown Jewels is the most valuable set of jewellery in the world.

Cullinan

This was the largest rough diamond ever found. It was found in a South African **mine** in 1905. It weighed over 3,000 carats before it was cut into 105 gems. The largest gem cut from it is a 530-carat stone called the Cullinan I. Today it is part of the Crown Jewels.

Hope

This 45-carat diamond is a striking blue colour. It was once part of a larger diamond called the Great Blue. Today, it is housed in the National Museum of Natural History in Washington, D.C., USA.

Golden Jubilee

This is the largest cut diamond in the world today, weighing 545 carats. The stone is yellowish-brown. In 1997 it was given to the king of Thailand to honour his 50 years as king.

Dresden Green

This very rare gem is the largest and finest green diamond ever found. It is cut in the shape of an almond and weighs over 40 carats.

◀ British artist Damien Hirst covered a platinum cast of a human skull in 8,601 diamonds. Valued at £50 million, it is said to be the most expensive piece of modern-day art.

Timeline

(These dates are often approximations.)

2 to 3 billion years ago

Diamonds form in the **mantle** of Earth; they later explode onto the surface through ancient volcanoes.

3 BYA

1300s

European **royalty** wear small diamonds in jewellery.

1200s

King Louis IX of France passes a law saying only the king can wear diamonds.

1000

1477

Emperor Maximilian I gives a diamond wedding ring to wife Mary, Duchess of Burgundy.

1500s

Royal jewellery begins to feature larger diamonds; jewellers begin putting **facets** on diamonds.

1500

1893

French scientist Henri Moissan examines rock samples from a **meteor** and discovers moissanite.

1889

Rhodes buys the Kimberley Mining Company; he names the new company De Beers.

1905

The Cullinan diamond is found in a South African mine; it is the largest rough diamond ever found, weighing over 3,000 carats.

1900   **1925**

1997

The king of Thailand receives the Golden Jubilee diamond to honour his 50 years as king.

1990s

Concern grows over **blood diamonds**.

2000

Thieves try but fail to steal 12 diamonds from the Millennium Dome in London.

2002

The United States and other countries agree to end the sale of blood diamonds.

2000

28

 This symbol shows where there is a change of scale in the timeline, or where a long period of time with no noted events has been left out.

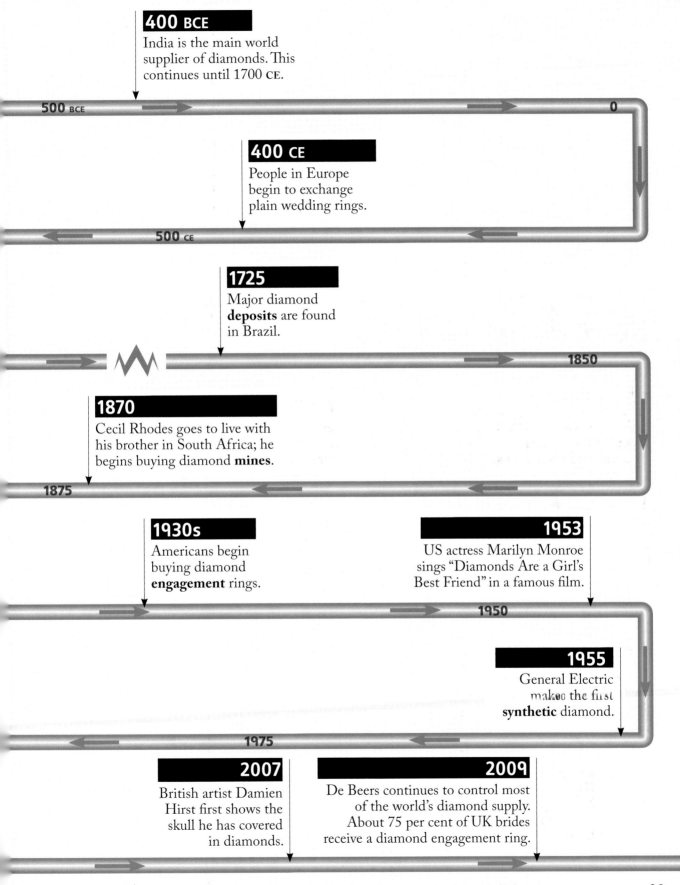

400 BCE
India is the main world supplier of diamonds. This continues until 1700 CE.

500 BCE

0

400 CE
People in Europe begin to exchange plain wedding rings.

500 CE

1725
Major diamond **deposits** are found in Brazil.

1850

1870
Cecil Rhodes goes to live with his brother in South Africa; he begins buying diamond **mines**.

1875

1930s
Americans begin buying diamond **engagement** rings.

1953
US actress Marilyn Monroe sings "Diamonds Are a Girl's Best Friend" in a famous film.

1950

1955
General Electric makes the first **synthetic** diamond.

1975

2007
British artist Damien Hirst first shows the skull he has covered in diamonds.

2009
De Beers continues to control most of the world's diamond supply. About 75 per cent of UK brides receive a diamond engagement ring.

Glossary

alluvial deposits made by flowing water. Alluvial diamonds are found in the banks of rivers and streams.

BCE meaning "before the common era". When this appears after a date, it refers to the time before the Christian religion began. BCE dates are always counted backwards.

blood diamond diamond that is mined in a country that has a corrupt (dishonest) government or that is controlled by violent groups

brilliance sparkle of a diamond. The brilliance of diamonds is beautiful.

carat measure of a diamond's weight. One carat weighs 0.2 of a gram (0.007 of an ounce).

carbon one of the most common substances on Earth. All plants, animals, and living things contain carbon.

CE meaning "common era". When this appears after a date, it refers to the time after the Christian religion began.

deposit build-up of substances by natural processes. Diamond deposits are found in many countries around the world.

emperor ruler similar to a king. Emperor Maximilian I ruled over a large area of Europe.

engagement agreement to get married. Often people give rings for a wedding engagement.

facet flat cut on the surface of a gem. Facets help more light pass through diamonds.

fancy diamond high-quality coloured diamond. Fancy diamonds are harder to find than clear ones.

fire coloured light a diamond gives off. Diamonds have the most fire of any gem.

gem stone that can be cut and polished to shine brightly

gem quality good enough to be used for jewellery

kimberlite bluish-grey rock formed by magma cooling in the ground. Kimberlite pipes often contain diamonds.

magma hot, melted rock from deep inside Earth. Ancient volcanoes spewed magma that carried diamonds.

mantle middle part of Earth about 195 kilometres (120 miles) below ground, between the crust and the core. Diamonds formed in the mantle about two to three billion years ago.

meteor rock from space that lands on Earth. Geologists examine rock from meteors.

mine pit or tunnel from which minerals (such as diamonds, coal, or gold) are taken; also, to dig a mine, to get something from a mine, or to work in a mine. The Big Hole mine in South Africa is a famous diamond mine.

royalty kings, queens, and members of the royal court. For many hundreds of years, diamonds were mostly worn by royalty.

scarce rare

synthetic made by humans. Today, scientists can make synthetic diamonds.

Find out more

Books

Resources: Gemstones and the Environment, Ian Mercer (Franklin Watts, 2004)

Rocks, Minerals, and Resources: Diamonds and Gemstones, Ron Edwards and Lisa Dickie (Crabtree, 2004)

Websites

This link leads to a film about the history of diamonds from the Natural History Museum.
http://www.nhm.ac.uk/nature-online/earth/rock-minerals/history-of-diamonds/index.html

Learn how diamonds formed and more on this PBS site.
www.pbs.org/wnet/nature/fun/diamonds_flash.html

Have a look at some famous diamonds on this site.
http://www.debeersgroup.com/en/About-diamonds/a-few-famous-diamonds/

Place to visit

Natural History Museum
Cromwell Road
London SW7 5BD
http://www.nhm.ac.uk/

Visit the Darwin Centre to view the Museum's gemstone collection.

Index